Holy Liturgy & Me

SAINT **SHENOUDA** PRESS

Holy Liturgy & Me

Fr Bishoy Kamel

Translated By
Yvonne Tadros

ST SHENOUDA PRESS
SYDNEY, AUSTRALIA
2021

Holy Liturgy and Me

Father Bishoy Kamel

COPYRIGHT © 2021
St Shenouda Press

ST SHENOUDA PRESS
8419 Putty Rd,
Putty, NSW, 2330
Sydney, Australia

www.stshenoudapress.com

ISBN 13: 978-0-6451395-0-1

Translated by:
Yvonne Tadros

Contents

Translator's Note:

These sermons were written in colloquial Egyptian Arabic. I tried my best to translate them for the English reader according to English sentence structure, with adherence to meaning in the Arabic version and at the same time reflecting the spirituality therein, as this booklet is part of a series of sermons by the Rev. Hegumenos Bishoy Kamel. Proper nouns are transliterated. There may also be spelling variations.

Biblical Quote References are from NIV or NKJV depending on which is closest to the Arabic Version.

What is the Divine Liturgy?

PRIEST'S PRAYER IN THE LITURGY

O' God, You loved us in order that You endowed us with the grace that we may be called Your children, sharing in Your gifts and Fatherhood:

May You purify our inner nature which we pray to partake of, the kind of purity being found only in the human nature of Your Son.

We beseech You to:

• Cast away from us any adulterous and profane thoughts; we seek this in the name of Him who was born of a pure Virgin.

• Cast away from us all arrogance; we seek this in the name of Him who humbled Himself for our sake.

• Cast away from us all fear; we seek this in the name of Him who suffered in the flesh and demonstrated the power of the cross.

• Cast away from us all vainglory; we seek this in the name of Him who was struck and scourged for our sake, and did not turn away His face from the shame of spitting.

• Cast away from us all sins and thoughts of envy, killing, straying and hatred; we seek this in the name of the Lamb of God who carried away the sins of the world.

• Cast away from us anger and the harbouring of evil thoughts; we seek this in the name of Him who was nailed on the cross for our sins.

• Cast away from us the works of Satan and all demons; we seek this in the name of Him who scattered and defeated the powers of evil and darkness.

• Cast away from us all evil thoughts; we seek this in the name of Him who ascended into Heaven.

We ask You to make us worthy to partake in this sacrament in purity and perfection from our bodies and spirits. Thus, we may partake of You in thanksgiving.

WITHOUT THIS SACRAMENT,
WE CANNOT SURVIVE

"Christians raise the sacrament of the Eucharist and the sacrament of the Eucharist raises them. No one can survive without the Eucharist." (Martyrs of Carthage)

"The sacrifice of the Divine Liturgy is the ultimate sacrifice for which God created the world" (Maximos the Confessor)

With these profound thoughts, we shall walk through the path that seeks life through the Divine Mystery of the Eucharist

WHY DID CHRIST OFFER HIMSELF
ON THE EVE OF HIS CRUCIFIXION?

First: The ultimate act of love is sacrifice until death.

God demonstrated his love of mankind through several means; through His sweet words, healing of the sick, resurrection of the dead and finally when He offered his body broken for the remission of sins and eternal life to those who partake of Him, "It was just before the Passover Festival. Jesus knew that the hour had come for him to leave this world and go to the Father. Having loved his own who were in the world, he loved them to the end."(Jn 13:1)

God's love became tangible when He broke His body for us to receive remission of sins. Thus, the benefit of attending liturgy lies in our perception of the mystery contained in the sacrifice. It is the embodiment of the divine love, in which we witness His sacrifice for us being offered on the altar. John the Apostle said, "He loved them to the end."(Jn 13:1). It was the Lord's desire to sacrifice Himself, "I have eagerly desired to eat this Passover with you before I suffer" (Lk 22:15). Therefore, we ought to attend Liturgy with a desire for the Eucharist in which we receive the Lord's body, just like Christ's desire to sacrifice Himself for our sake. Worship during the liturgy should be a desire combined with love.

My Lord Jesus:

"Your desire led you to offer Yourself as a sacrifice for my sake, and my desire is to offer myself as a sacrifice for Your sake. Allow me to become food for the wild beasts, through whose means it will be granted me to reach God. I am the wheat of God, and am ground by the teeth of the wild beasts, that I may be found the pure bread of Christ ." (St. Ignatius)

<u>At St. Demiana's grave:</u>

When we offered the divine sacrifice on the altar erected on St. Demiana's grave, a thought occurred to me that was a depiction of the image in the book of Revelation, "And when he had opened the fifth seal, I saw under the altar the souls of them that were slain for the word of God, and for the testimony which they held"(Rev 6:9).

The martyrs literally experienced the sacrifice of Christ on the cross. They bowed their heads before being slaughtered for the sake of Him who offered his life as a sacrifice for our sake. Thus though we have the altar of Christ who performed the ultimate sacrifice, we also have the relics of the martyrs that constitute the basis of the altar.

<u>Second: To reveal the secret image of The Lord</u>

The Lord lived as a friend among his disciples and then his physical body disappeared from their lives so that they would become His invisible body. During the last supper with his disciples, He offered His body and blood to be given for the remission of sins. Though He may have physically disappeared from his disciples, they became His invisible body. He is no longer on earth as a visible body but as the one body of the Church.

At the end of the Eucharist, when the physical body disappears from the altar, it remains within us because 'we are his invisible body'. For this reason, Christ's body needs to completely disappear from the altar - not a jewel is to be left - according to the rites of our beloved church.

The feeling of the congregation during communion is one that 'we are His invisible body' and also one of the martyrs said, 'No one can survive without the Eucharist'.

The Church eats the body and drinks the blood

Partaking in drinking the blood of Christ is constant purification to enable us to acquire purity and be a member of Christ's pure church.

The body of Christ broken for the church is His 'Invisible Body' carrying the cross, while the church partakes in the body which was slain for the whole world. The church unites the earthly with the heavenly where Christ is present. This has been revealed in the form of the slain lamb, "Then I saw a Lamb, looking as if it had been slain, standing at the center of the throne..."(Rev 5:6)

The Church is the Body of Christ (Corpus Christi)

"Your people and your Church pray to you and the Father through you ...."

Through Christ and in Him, we pray to our God the Father. On earth, Christ took our visible body, and upon His ascension to Heaven He called us to be members of His invisible body. Thus, being such members, we pray through Him and in Him as He is the Head of this body.

In His farewell prayer, the Lord Jesus prayed on behalf of mankind saying "Father......". Then, when He gave us the Holy

Spirit and His sacred body, we pray to the Father during the liturgy saying, "have mercy upon us…". We seek His intercession for the sick, peace, and rivers…

As we being members of Christ's body, His divine final farewell prayer was fulfilled in us, "And in that day you will ask Me nothing. Most assuredly, I say to you, whatever you ask the Father in My name He will give you. Until now you have asked nothing in My name. Ask, and you will receive, that your joy may be full. These things I have spoken to you in figurative language; but the time is coming when I will no longer speak to you in figurative language, but I will tell you plainly about the Father. In that day you will ask in My name, and I do not say to you that I shall pray the Father for you; for the Father Himself loves you, because you have loved Me, and have believed that I came forth from God." (Jn 16:23-27)

Immediately upon the invocation of the Holy Spirit upon the bread and wine, the priest says, "Lord, let us all be worthy of receiving your Holies so as to be one body and one spirit with all your saints."

<u>I am a member of the body</u>

We eat the body of the crucified Lord as seen in the bible, "and when He had given thanks, He broke it and said, "Take, eat: this is My body, which is broken for you: do this in remembrance of Me." (1 Cor 11:24)

Our partnership during the Liturgy is one with the slain Christ. For this reason the Church carries the cross of Christ being fed from the body which was slain for the whole world.

CHRIST'S INVISIBLE BODY
ENDURES SUFFERINGS

1. The members in the body of Christ suffer while fighting until death against the sins of the world. Examples include the martyrs and confessors, and the sufferings of those who go through spiritual wars against the powers of evil and whose sufferings are shared with the heavenlies. The book of Isaiah says, "In all their affliction he was afflicted, and the angel of his presence saved them:"(Is 63:9)

2. The sufferings of the spiritually ailing members whose illnesses develop into malignant worldly desires. The invisible body and its head carry those burdens of severe sufferings, in addition to the sins and all other evils.

The Christian is a member of Christ's suffering body. He carries his cross behind the crucified Jesus who carried His cross saying, "If anyone desires to come after Me, let him deny himself and take up his cross daily, and follow me." (Lk 9:23)

<u>What if I avoid carrying the cross?</u>

This concept creates great fear in me...because it means one's detachment from the body of the crucified Christ, i.e., the Church who was crucified for the sake of the world. St. Paul said, "But God forbid that I should glory, save in the cross of our Lord Jesus Christ, by whom the world is crucified unto me, and I unto the world." (Gal 6:14)

Therefore the cross is my life and without it I am detached

from the crucified body. "Who is weak, and I am not weak? who is offended, and I burn not?" (2 Cor 11:29) I feed on the crucified body who was led like a lamb to the slaughter and for whose sake I wish to offer myself as a sacrifice for the obedience of His Gospel and commandments. One member of the body of Christ also sacrifices for the sake of Christ's mission and to let the sign of His cross be within me throughout my entire actions. "...for I bear in my body the marks of the Lord Jesus" (Gal 6:17)

When I pray, I place my hands in the shape of the cross, similar to when Moses held up his hands when he had overcome Amalek. In my case as a priest, there is a cross on the front of my altar vestments and another one at the back. The former is my cross, the latter is the cross of those I serve.

The meaning of "Humility"

I am not the one who exists, but rather I am a living member in Christ, the head of the Church Body - there is no independent entity for me. I can only function through the Head who moves me. "...created in Christ Jesus for good works, which God prepared beforehand that we should walk in them."(Eph 2:10)

Pride and a large ego are very dangerous as they result in the detachment from Christ's Body. The person is proud is cut off from the true vine, no longer being a branch attached to the tree. This is what takes place when one is immersed in the 'ego'.

EGOISM: is detachment from the true vine, the head

HUMILITY: represents a branch firmly attached to Christ's Body

SELF-DENIAL: is real attachment to Christ. It is the denial of the 'self' so that the branch may thrive in the vine, in union with other members. This is the only access to humility.

The Meaning of Intercession

All the members of Christ's body are united together. If one member suffers, all the other members suffer; if one is honoured, all the other members share in the joy. These feelings originate from the firm union of the members within Christ's body and this is the meaning of "intercession" according to our beloved church.

Whenever one is immersed in the love of Christ, one's feelings unite with those of others: such as the poor and the rich, the old and the young,... etc. As these feelings deepen, it is an indication of the strong unity in Christ's body.

An example of the greatness of intercession was Abba Abram, Bishop of Al-Fayoum who sensed the individual needs of his parish without discrimination. Thus during his lifetime on earth, he was an intercessor, and still a great intercessor in heaven.

Prayers of the departed: those who deny the prayers of the departed separate themselves from Christ's body who unites all with all.

The meaning of Love

Love is when one is connected to Christ's body. It is being

firmly connected to the true vine, together with the other branches. As for those who are weak and hold a different opinion, they are nevertheless in need to join the true vine. The physiology of the church body necessitates that no organ can survive without the other, and if there are sick organs they hurt the whole body.... Therefore, these need to be healed, connecting them with the rest to enjoy the peace and happiness of Christ, the Lord.

<u>You and I are the light of the world</u>

The Lord Jesus is the only true light. Christ said, "I am the light of the world."(Jn 8:12). Once a person becomes a member of His body, he becomes the light of the world through Him. "You are the light of the world"(Mt 5:14) For this reason, the Lord said that while we are on earth we are the light of the world, and when we go to Heaven we will join the righteous saying, "Then the righteous will shine like the sun in the kingdom of their Father."(Mt 13:43)

<u>The Holy Spirit confirms us in Christ's body</u>

•Through the Holy Spirit we are born in baptism and consecrated by the Holy Myron, whereby all our organs are consecrated in Christ who purifies us. He helps us to repent and enables us to receive His body in the Eucharist. "We know it by the Spirit he gave us" (1 Jn 3:24).

•The Holy Spirit takes of what is Christ unto us. Christ anoints "But you have an anointing from the Holy One, and all of you know the truth."(1 Jn 2:20) We become blessed with the Holy Spirit when we say "Our Abba, our Father...." - "In the same way, the Spirit helps us in our weakness. We do not know what we ought to pray for, but the Spirit himself intercedes for us through wordless groans. And he who searches our hearts knows the mind of the Spirit, because the Spirit intercedes for God's people in accordance with the will of God". (Rom 8:26)

He gives us what is His: this includes His Spirit, the force of His Resurrection, His purity, and His meekness. In other words, we are blessed by acquiring all that is Christ's.

•The Holy Spirit confirms and leads us to bear fruit for Christ, "Remain in me, as I also remain in you. No branch can bear fruit by itself; it must remain in the vine. Neither can you bear fruit unless you remain [in me]" (Jn 15:4).

•The Holy Spirit is the one who resurrects the dead members and confirms them, "But if the Spirit of Him who raised Jesus from the dead dwells in you, He who raised Christ from the dead will also give life to your mortal bodies." (Rom 8:11)

•The Holy Spirit is the one who offers us the body of the Lord Jesus on the altar. He offers Christ's body to the Church being its nurture throughout our exile on this earth.

Finally, my beloved, let us always strive towards being firm members in His body. AMEN.

THE LITURGY

LINK WITH HEAVEN

While the beloved Apostle John was in exile on the island of Patmos, he witnessed a heavenly liturgical scene. The altar contained a living sacrifice, a lamb that was slain, which were the souls of the martyrs. There were angelic priests, angels, and incense offered as the prayers of saints. Thus, this great mystery was revealed. The Liturgical sacrifice enables us to have a view of Heaven whereby we break the barriers of time and space and become attached to eternity. We become triumphant and free of shackles.

The Divine Liturgy makes present among us the mystery of the incarnation on the cross, His resurrection and the waiting for His second coming, "The Incomprehensible has been touched, and the Unseen has been seen, and the Son of the living God, truly became the Son of man".

When God saw that man on earth was longing for Heaven, He gave him His precious body and blood on earth to connect to Heaven, "When we stand before your holy altar, may we be counted among those standing in Heaven".

Heaven and mankind, the sublime versus the lowly.... Is there a common factor between them?

It is only there within your heart, O' Lord Jesus, while you are on the cross, that the connection co-exists between these opposites? It is here on the altar, Heaven and mankind in your presence? "For so God loved the world, that He gave us His own Son" (John 3:16)

Reflections

• The Divine Liturgy is the greatest work which takes place in our life. The body of Christ is present among us before whom angels bow and demons tremble before His holy name.

• The Liturgy is not merely reciting words of prayer, but rather the tool and means towards a greater purpose. The Holy Spirit is present during the Liturgy to sanctify the sacrifice.

During the Liturgy are the congregation are together in heart and prayer, like an orchestra, following the same melodious tune of Christ dead but alive. It is the melody of love and self-denial, the melody of forgiveness through the shedding of blood, the melody of eternal life.

The sanctuary is full of the multitudes of angels and saints, and at its doorsteps are large numbers seeking healing, such as those who are sick, lame or paraplegic waiting for a cure. The sick are not near the pool of Bethesda but before the sanctuary of the Lord of Hosts... The members of the church are not waiting for merely an angel but rather the Creator of angels... We are all suffering from all types of ailments (whether mild or severe). For example, the Magdalene who suffered from lust, or Peter who rashly denied Christ, or the one who suffered from fear like Nicodemus who met Jesus only at night, or he who suffers from greed like Zacchaeus or the right hand thief crucified with Christ and many others. The congregation, like these biblical characters, moan and groan awaiting their healing through the sacrifice of the lamb, seeking redemption and life.

The Church is a hospital for the body, soul and spirit. This is mentioned in the prayer of the sick, "Take away from them, and from us, every sickness and every malady; the spirit of sickness, chase away. Those who are long lain in maladies, raise up and comfort. Those who are afflicted by unclean spirits, set them all free...O You, the true physician of our souls and bodies, the Bishop of all flesh, visit us with Your salvation."

The divine liturgy is therefore the hospital where God does not punish sinners but grants forgiveness.

Participation of angels in the Liturgy

• At the beginning of the liturgy of the faithful, the deacon says, "Raise your eyes towards the east to see the altar with the body and blood of our God Emmanuel laid on it, where angels and archangels stand by, covering their faces before the brightness of the greatness of His glory...."

• The Priest announces the presence of the angels by their nine ranks and participation in prayers, "Before whom stand the angels, the archangels, the principalities, the authorities, the thrones, the dominions and the powers...You are He around whom stand the cherubim full of eyes, and the seraphim with six wings, praising continuously, without ceasing saying"

St. Theodore states, "The two deacons standing next to the altar represent the two angels who stood next to the tomb at the resurrection. The altar represents the tomb because on it or within it the sacrifice is placed." St. Theodore also says that a deacon stands next to the sacrifice representing the angel who came to the Lord in the garden of Gethsemane offering comfort when Christ was going through the agony of the sacrifice. The sacrifice in the liturgy is the very suffering of the Lord's sacrifice.

• At the conclusion of the Liturgy the priest asks the attending angel ascending to heaven to remember those present to the Lord, which is similar to the angel who carried the prayers of Cornelius to heaven.

The communion of angels
and our communion with them

Glory to our God who, through His incarnation and sacrifice on the cross, reconciled the heavenly with the earthly, uniting both into one:

•The angels: "....and they rest not day and night, saying, Holy, holy, holy, Lord God Almighty, ...(Rev 4:8) - "And they were calling to one another: "Holy, holy, holy is the LORD Almighty; the whole earth is full of his glory." (Is 6:3)

St. Cyril of Jerusalem states that, "it is for this reason we recite this praise"

Also, St. Chrysostom says ".... all the heavenly armies attend and chant this praise and the altar is filled with angels in honour of the sacrifice. All the angels pray together with the priest... The spiritual flame of the Holy Spirit descends from heaven; the blood comes from the side of the pure lamb into the chalice to purify our souls."

"What right have you got O' Christian that you dare to disrespectfully stand before this sacrifice... The church is the real heaven". He also adds "... The offering of the sacrifice is the most appropriate time to ask God.... Even angels take the opportunity of this joyful moment to praise God for the countless blessings and fervently beseech Him for our sake"

•The Church calls the saints "earthly angels" or "heavenly beings". Also, as an expression of the angelic nature of saints, the Coptic Iconographer paints the icons of some saints with six wings similar to the Seraphim, such as St. Tekla Hemanout.

•When we stand for prayer during the morning prayer we say, "Let us praise with the angels saying 'Glory to God in the highest, peace on earth and good will toward men.'"

The vigilance of
the angels in the Liturgy

• St. John the short witnessed the protection of angels during the Liturgy. He once described an angel holding a sword protecting those who came to pray and enter church... Truly all the angels help those who come for prayer, "there will be more rejoicing in heaven over one sinner who repents..." (Lk 15:7)

• Angels raise prayers and sacrifices to heaven... In the litany of the oblations the priest says, "receive these through the service of your holy angels and archangels"

• Angels love us to such an extent that they "They send up the hymn of victory and salvation which is ours, with a voice full of glory" (Gregorian Liturgy)

The Gregorian Liturgy mentions the praise in the book of Revelation as being "the praise of triumph and of our salvation in voices full of glory".

 "Now when He had taken the scroll, the four living creatures and the twenty-four elders fell down before the Lamb, each having a harp, and golden bowls full of incense, which are the prayers of the saints. And they sang a new song, saying: "You are worthy to take the scroll, And to open its seals; For You were slain, And have redeemed us to God by Your blood Out of every tribe and tongue and people and nation" (Rev 5:8-9).

How do we stand amongst angels?

1 Since the Liturgy of the faithful commences with the presence of the angels, the priest announces the presence of the Lord by saying, "The Lord be with you" and then "Lift up your hearts...." The congregation respond, "they are with the Lord". Hence, since the angels cover their faces in awe, we also ought to lift up our hearts to the Lord in the same reverence.

The Liturgy is intended for us to stand before God; it is being in the presence of the Holy Trinity. Thus, a priest who is lax while officiating in the Liturgy deprives his soul and the church from honouring and glorifying the Holy Trinity.

2 The praise of the angels rotates around the word "HOLY". Without Holiness we are unable to see the Lord, nor participate in the liturgical sacrifice. God is Holy and we ought to be Holy. Through what number of tears are we to seek and strive for holiness? The Liturgy is the assembly of the sanctified people together with those sanctified angels in the presence of the Holy Lord .... "The Holies are for the Holies."

• In the Liturgy of St. Cyril he says, "... In the same way You purified the lips of your servant Prophet Isaiah as described by him "...one of the seraphim flew to me, having in his hand a live coal which he had taken with the tongs from the altar. And he touched my mouth with it, and said: "Behold, this has touched your lips; Your iniquity is taken away, And your sin purged." Thus, also we are weak standing before You seeking Your mercy and say, "Come O' Lord, purify our souls, bodies, lips and our hearts. Give us this ember which gives life to the soul, body and the spirit which is Your sacred body and blood"

3 Angels are humble as opposed to Satan who is arrogant. The angels cover their faces, praising in fear and reverence. Thus, whoever attends the Liturgy together with the angels listens to the deacon's command, "Stand up in the fear of God.... Bow your heads before The Lord"

Humility was exemplified in the prayer of the tax collector. His spirit was an example of how we should come to the Liturgy. According to the Didascalia, the deacon and the psaltos should not be singing boastfully, nor should they sing in loud voices but rather in awe and reverence similar to the angels.

CONDITIONS FOR PARTICIPATING IN THE LITURGY

Attending Liturgy is not merely standing physically in the Church, but rather communion with the angels, saints, congregation and the Lord Jesus. Liturgy is communion in His sacrifice, power and triumph of His Resurrection. Only those who share in the love, death and resurrection of the Lord are in communion with the church in one heart.

For those who recall the "Veil and Reconciliation Prayers", which precedes the liturgy of the faithful, one finds that the church draws the attention of the congregation to two very important factors:

• Loving one another

• Contrition and great humility of our sins, magnified by God's intense and innumerable love for us.

FIRST: Loving one another:

The Liturgy of the faithful commences with the Reconciliation Prayer saying, "Lord, make all of us worthy of kissing each other a holy kiss so that we may not be cast unto judgment...." The deacon also calls upon the congregation to, "kiss each other in holiness". Thus:

1. It is vividly clear that love is the first prerequisite to be in communion with the Lord during the Liturgy. Whoever participates in communion with the Eucharist without a sincere and loving heart is in danger of falling into condemnation. The Lord gave us a warning saying, "Therefore, if you are offering your gift at the altar and there remember that your brother or sister has something against you, leave your gift there in front of the altar. First go and be reconciled to them; then come and offer your gift."(Mt.5:23-24). Leaving the offering on the altar is a thousand times better than participating in Liturgy while being under subject to judgment.

2. The Divine Liturgy originates from God's love towards us.

One should ask if the hymns of the Liturgy reach our hearts? As an analogy, in order to hear something on the radio the receiver needs to be tuned to the same wavelength of the transmitter. This is the case with whoever participates in the Liturgy... One will not taste the sweetness of the lamb unless their hearts are attuned to the same wavelength of love emitted by the transmitter, the divine sacrifice on the altar.

The whole Church ought to be immersed in a sea of love; the Bishop, the Priest, the Deacons and the Congregation should all sing the hymns of the Liturgy, which stem from the Christ who offered Himself for our sake.

3. Love is the strongest channel used by the Holy Spirit to firmly join members in the body of Christ. This is the way the Holy Spirit provides the impetus towards having fervent prayers.

Love is a result of a united heart. During the Liturgy the church fervently prays for the patriarch, the bishops, the deacons, all the servants, the safety of the place, the salvation of the whole congregation, the married, the celibate, the elderly, the youth, the rich, the poor, the fallen, the upright and all those who have not been mentioned. The priest concludes by saying, "and bless your people, O Lord, with the oneness of heart..."

In summary, the deacon's call to love before the commencement of the Liturgy of the faithful consists of:

•Whoever participates in the Liturgy without love may be subject to judgment. The heart which is void of love will not attract, nor reap any benefit from attending the Liturgy.

•The Liturgy is a sacrificial offering.

•The third and vital factor is that the holy Liturgy is the communion of all the loving members of the one body. Based on this concept, the main target of the church becomes living within the spring of love. For each church servant, irrespective of their status within the church, unity becomes the greatest priority... The oneness of heart is mentioned throughout the Liturgy.

Therefore, my beloved, if love is the means of our union with the divine sacrifice of love, let us examine our hearts and join in the liturgical prayer, "Clean us from all blemish, all guile, all hypocrisy, all craftiness, and the remembrance of evil entailing death. And make us all worthy, O our Master, to greet one another with a holy kiss, that, without casting us into condemnation, we may partake of Your immortal and heavenly gift in Christ Jesus our Lord."

SECOND: Standing with Contrition

"Two men went up to the temple to pray, one a Pharisee and the other a tax collector. The Pharisee stood and prayed thus with himself, 'God, I thank You that I am not like other men-extortioners, unjust, adulterers, or even as this tax collector. I fast twice a week; I give tithes of all that I possess.' And the tax collector, standing afar off, would not so much as raise his eyes to heaven, but beat his breast, saying, 'God, be merciful to me a sinner!' I tell you, this man went down to his house justified rather than the other;" (Lk 18:9-14) - This parable provides a framework of how Jesus taught us to pray when we stand before Him.

The Church teaches us to be repentant when the deacon says, "Bow your heads" while the congregation respond "Here we are, before You O Lord, in submission...."

Today, all Church members need to examine their standing before God during the Liturgy. How can one do this?

1. Contrition: is an outcome of examining oneself, similar to the tax collector rather than the Pharisee who compared himself to others. When I examine myself, I will realize that my 'ego' is the biggest obstacle which can separate myself from God. I will see that my heart is full of arrogance, selfishness, impurity, love of the worldly....

•"My Lord Jesus, as from today, I will see that when I stand before You, I will stand at a distance because You are pure. I shall bow my head in humility before your bountiful love. I will beat my chest in repentance because I am in need of Your mercy upon my unclean heart... I stand before You in fear and awe."

2. Contrition: is an outcome reflecting God's bountiful love in contrast with my many sins and unworthiness when I receive the Lord's pure body living a life full of evil, lust and lukewarmness.

3. Contrition: is a fierce battle with my 'ego'. No more should I say 'I', but rather "Christ who is alive within me" I will say "I have been crucified with Christ; it is no longer I who live, but Christ lives in me; and the life which I now live in the flesh I live by faith in the Son of God, who loved me and gave Himself for me." (Gal 2:20) The battle of dealing with the 'ego' will constantly motivate me to repent in order to receive the

Holy of the Holies, since without holiness no-one is able to see the Lord.

4. Contrition: is an outcome of feeling in need:

• A strong need for the divine blood to wash my soul from impurity.

• A need to partake of the sacred body to live and be able to mysteriously unite with Him.

• A need to partake in the blood of Christ and enjoy the overflow of the spring of love, "If you knew the gift of God......"

MY LORD

•I am the "...wretched, pitiful, poor, blind and naked."(Rev. 3:17) I, hereby, stand before you like a beggar who is invited to the banquet of the wealthy. I ask for the gold that is purified by fire to make be cleansed, and white clothing to cover me from the shame of my nakedness and kohl for my eyes so that I may see.

MY LORD

•You dwell in the highest and look upon the humble. If I am not humble during the Liturgy, You will not look upon me. Lord, please forgive my lukewarmness and kindle the fire of Your love in my heart. Forgive my blindness and let the light of Your presence shine upon my life. Look upon my poverty that as from today, may You be my only comfort. Let all my feelings and whole heart be drawn to You so that You become my only concern. I am a worthless worm, a rotten dog but through You I become Your beautiful fragrance.

MY LORD

•You allowed me to touch Your body and partake of it... How is this possible? What about this hand that touches You? The mouth which receives You? The eyes which look at You?

•"We ask You, O our Master, turn us not back when we put our hands on this awesome and bloodless sacrifice. For we put no trust in our righteousness, but in Your mercy, whereby You have given life to our race... unto the wiping of our sins and the forgiveness of our negligence" (Veil Prayer - St. Basil)

•"I am not worthy to serve You... Do not cast me away, and do not turn Your face away from me. Please erase all my faults, wash all the impurities of my soul and purify me totally" (Veil Prayer - St. Gregory)

•"I, being helpless and weak, beseech You, O mighty Lord..." (Veil Prayer - St. Cyril)

•"Purify our lips and release our minds from the evil thoughts of the devil" (Reconciliation Prayer - St. John Chrysostom")

•You as God, are a consuming fire. Because of Your ineffable condescension and love toward mankind, You did not burn the guileful traitor when he drew near to You, but greeted him with the greeting of fellowship, drawing him unto repentance and the recognition of his presumptuousness (Reconciliation Prayer - St. Severus)

Thus the whole church stands in remorse and contrition during the Liturgy seeking the Father saying, "Have mercy upon us, O God our Saviour"

In conclusion, my beloved children, each time we enter the church in the presence of God during the Liturgy, let us remember that we should not attend the Liturgy of the faithful unless we are reconciled to each other in a truly contrite and pure heart, standing before God in fear and awe.

THE POWER OF THE
LORD'S BODY AND BLOOD

"On the night The Lord Jesus was betrayed, He took bread and upon giving thanks, He broke it and said, "This is my body, which is for you; do this in remembrance of me." In the same way, after supper he took the cup, saying, "This cup is the new covenant in my blood; do this, whenever you drink it, in remembrance of me" For whenever you eat this bread and drink this cup, you proclaim the Lord's death until he comes (1 Cor 11:26).

Truly the body of Christ is offered on the altar, inviting us to be in communion with His suffering and crucified body. We can say, "remember His holy sufferings...." and continue praying: " .... we now offer you Your sacred sacrifice ...."

Christ's death on the cross is powerful, His crucified body bears life for the believers. Thus, each time we partake of the Lord's body we ought to do so with a strong belief in His power.

FIRST: The Power of the Sacrifice

We have received the power of Christ's sacrifice through baptism, "Therefore we are buried with him by baptism into death...."(Rom 6:4) and which we renew daily through repentance and confession in communion with His body, crucified for our sins. Thus, we ought to always come forward in faith to acquire the power of the dying Lord within our mortal bodies, "Always bearing about in the body the dying of the Lord Jesus, that the life also of Jesus might be made manifest in our body."(2 Cor 4:10)

In relation to the world, we hold within us the crucified body dead to the world saying, " ...by whom the world is crucified unto me, and I unto the world."(Gal 6:14). This is the main purpose of communion: to acquire the mystery of the power of death through the Lord's crucified body. Partaking of holy communion should lead to the death of the ego, especially when can be carried away by people's praise or affected by criticism. It is the death of lust, being judgmental and of worldly attachments.

We acclaim joyfully "Amen, Amen, Amen, we proclaim Your death O, Lord..."

• The power of dying with Christ is entirely different to being suppressed and deprived.

When one is suppressed, it creates feelings of anxiety and weakness; this struggle ends in breaking down a person. In contrast, the power of dying with Christ creates feelings of strength, triumph and joy. It is the beginning of Christ living within us. A contemporary Father described, "the moment of the offering of the Sacrament is an awesome mystery - it is the moment of the meeting between death and life. A Christian understands this concept from the parable of the grain of wheat as described by Christ our Lord."

• The amount of benefit from the mysterious power of Christ's sacrifice depends on our acknowledgement of the effects that corruption and death have on our body. One should acknowledge that his place during the Liturgy is among adulterers, sinners and thieves. As a matter of fact, it is the beginning of discovering the crucified Christ on the altar, "Therefore I take pleasure in infirmities, in reproaches, in necessities, in persecutions, in distresses for Christ's sake: for when I am weak, then am I strong."(2 Cor 12:10)

• Saints are people who are well aware of their weaknesses and limitations. Their major virtue is that they persevere and offer all that they have towards Christ. Clearly, they realise their physical mortality and seek God to become united with His broken body. They partake in the Lord's death and through His power detach themselves from the world.

SECOND: The intimacy of crucifying one's will in Christ

In the Gregorian Liturgy, the priest addresses the Lord Jesus, "You came to the slaughter as a lamb even to the cross". He follows this by saying, "I offer you, my Lord, my free will and my deeds according to Your precepts". This supplication of the priest towards the Lord Jesus reveals the manner of participation with Christ during the liturgy. The priest offers himself, or in other words, he is offering his will and all his deeds to walk alongside Christ as an obedient lamb submitting to the Father's will in communion with Him who is being led to the slaughter.

It is the equation in line with the teachings of the Gospel, "I offer you, my Lord, my free will and my deeds...." is equivalent to "crucifying myself" and "... I offer you my deeds according to Your precepts" is equivalent to the Gospel's fellowship "until death"

•Our communion with the crucified body of Christ on the altar is uniting with Christ in Gethsemane "... not as I will, but as You will." Also, uniting with Him on the cross "Father, into your hands I commit my spirit."

The second power we acquire through holy communion is the power of crucifying our will together with Christ, who is driven to the slaughter on the altar.

THIRD: Communion with Christ's suffering for others

Once you believe that the sacrifice on the altar is on behalf of sinners throughout the world, you cannot help ask yourself, "How can I partake in this body without having the same love of the Lord? The same love that He had towards sinners whom He loved until death... Those who are far from God, those who disowned Him on the night of His sufferings, those who blasphemed Him, who stabbed and crucified Him yet He prayed for them seeking His Father's forgiveness and excused them for not knowing what they were doing!? "

• LORD, from now on we will train ourselves to live with You, to share in Your love towards mankind so that we can become truly worthy of partaking Your body. We will answer Your call in Gethsemane to remain with You. After supper, we will spend the night with You in Gethsemane for the sake of the whole world: those in the Church, at work, in colleges, in trains, in places of sin.... We will look at each one through Your own weeping eyes and through Your own body which was wounded for our sake, because whoever participates in

Your broken body ought to also share in Your sufferings.

<u>FOURTH: We also acclaim the death</u>

"The death of the Lord for our sake," is the offering of the Lamb who died for our sake in the Liturgy. The priest affirms the death of the Lord for our sake and is "given on our behalf as a salvation and forgiveness of sins and eternal life to whoever partakes of Him…" We earnestly yearn to drink Christ's blood to wash away our sins, thus, acclaiming the Lord's death. The church is the place where sinners meet with Christ who was crucified so that they may be forgiven. Also, the church members acclaim the Lord's death saying, "You are Christ who was stabbed in His side with a spear on Golgotha in Jerusalem, for our sake. You are the Lamb of God who takes away the sins of the world, forgive us our sins and trespasses, place us on your right hand." The church members continue praying, "Purify our lips O' Lord as You purified Isaiah's lips when one of the seraphim flew to him, having in his hand a live coal which he had taken with the tongs from the altar. And the seraphim touched Isaiah's mouth with it saying, "Behold, this has touched your lips; Your iniquity is taken away, your sin purged." (Is 6:7)

The priest continues, "Now Lord, give us this lifegiving body for our soul, the true live coal which is the Holy Body and the precious Blood."

This is the concept with which we attend Liturgy to acquire the fiery purification bestowed by the live coal of the divine body crucified for us.

FIFTH: We acknowledge Your Resurrection

For each soul that goes through death in Christ, the Lord will bestow upon him the power of His Resurrection with the living Christ. "For we who live are always delivered to death for Jesus' sake, that the life of Jesus also may be manifested in our mortal flesh." (2 Cor 4:11). The broken body on the altar bears the power of the Resurrection and only those who partake in it will feel His power... "I have been crucified with Christ; it is no longer I who live, but Christ lives in me;" (Gal 2:20) Death to the world is the beginning of our Resurrection in Christ.

It is impossible for a Christian to proclaim the resurrection of Christ unless one proclaims the power of death in Christ. This is the most profound mystery of the Eucharist: the mystery of mysteries in Christ. The Eucharist is the merging of life and death in the sacrament of Baptism, repentance and communion of the crucified Lord.

SIXTH: Finally, – We remember the Lord's second coming

We commemorate the Lord's second coming, not merely by words but by partaking of His Body and Blood. The Church lives at all times with Christ, nurtured by His body, penetrating the spheres of time and space in a permanent state with Christ. This is the meaning of the Church awaiting the Lord's second coming.

REFLECTIONS DURING COMMUNION

The Journey of my Life with Christ

1. Towards Gethsemane

Gethsemane is where I share the Lord's sufferings for the sake of the world and sinners. I stay with Him late at night, while He endures the sorrow leading to His death.

Now, I am about to partake of His body and drink His blood from the same cup my brethren are drinking from.

2. On the path of Him carrying the cross

The cross is where I walk with Christ to the slaughter the same way He did. "He was oppressed and afflicted, yet he did not open his mouth; he was led like a lamb to the slaughter, and as a sheep before its shearers is silent" (Is 53:7)

Now, I am about to receive the power of surrendering my free will and offering my deeds according to His precepts.

3. Towards Golgotha

Golgotha is where, on the cross, I receive the power over death. Now, I am about to receive His crucified body.

I am able to acclaim His power saying, "I am crucified with Christ". I am able to testify to the power of the cross"...through which the world has been crucified to me, and I to the world."

4. I see Him stabbed

On the cross Christ was stabbed. This is where I can drink the blood oozing from His side.

Now, I am washed from my sins. I am purified from all my iniquities. Also, I am healed from all my spiritual and physical illnesses.

5. I go to His tomb

Where I find the tomb empty, I proclaim the power of the Resurrection. Now, I am about to partake of His living body on the altar and Christ will dwell in me.

6. Finally, I go to Bethany

Where I see Him ascending on the cloud to heaven, I partake of His body and am attracted to Heaven until He takes me to ascend with Him on the cloud...AMEN

THE JOURNEY

ASCENT TO HEAVEN,
DESCENT TO THE WORLD

The church is the house of the Lord. We were reborn spiritually from above through baptism in the house of the Lord and soon after we were fed from the body of our Lord Jesus and given His blood to drink. These had been our stages throughout our exodus on Earth: we ascend daily towards the house of the Lord where we receive our sustenance to go out into the world.

Psalm 84 reveals the continuous ascension with God, "Blessed is the man whose strength is in You, Whose heart is set on pilgrimage. As they pass through the Valley of Baca....They go from strength to strength..."

The Lord took the disciples with Him and was transfigured on the high mountain. This heavenly transfiguration was were the disciples witnessed Christ's glory in the presence of Moses and Elijah. The disciples desired to remain with Him in this heavenly state forever.

The Journey of Ascension

1 Ascension is a longing and thirsting for Christ

Seeking the Lord wholeheartedly is a strong form of love described in the Song of Songs, "Sustain me with the cakes of raisins, Refresh me with apples, for I lovesick." (2:5) Yearning for God is reaching out in weakness and thirsting for Him, "O God, You are my God; Early will I seek You; My soul thirsts."(Ps 63:1). Clearly yearning is thirsting towards God Himself, "How lovely is your dwelling place, Lord Almighty! My soul yearns, even faints, for the courts of the Lord; my heart and my flesh cry out for the living God."(Ps 84:1) We live in this state of longing for the Lord while being outside the house of the Lord, "Even the sparrow has found a home, and the swallow a nest for herself, where she may have her young- a place near your altar, Lord Almighty, my King and my God". (Ps 84:3) Thus, we ought to have this intensive yearning towards God and a clear motive when ascending towards the Lord's Altar or during communion.

2 We ascend to offer the Eucharist to God

Liturgy of the Eucharist is the sacrament of thanksgiving. Thus, we thank Him for helping us through this hour, for He came and saved us. We kneel before Him filling us all with His joy and presence among us. Thus, we will never be worried and we thank him for all the blessings we receive... In other words, the whole liturgy is a sacrifice of thanksgiving.

3 Ascending is repentance and confirmation of our exodus on Earth

Ascending means being elevated above the futility and lusts of the world. One can say with King David, "He has founded his city on the holy mountain". (Ps 87:1) "I will lift up my eyes to the hills..." (Ps 121:1) On the way towards our ascent, we will find the Father ceaselessly running towards us to embrace and kiss us. The Son will be standing to wipe our tears and wash our feet with a towel around His waist. This is the state of the sacrament of repentance within the souls ascending towards the communion of the Lord's body.

Ascending towards God helps us realise the fact that we are foreigners in this world... However, despite the fact that we are alien to the world, during the liturgy we are in the arms of the Father in the house of the Lord.

<u>4 We ascend to eat so that we may live</u>
<u>and be steadfast in Him</u>

The world can only offer earthly food for the physical body…. The Lord's voice resonates in my ears, "Most assuredly, I say to you, unless you eat the flesh of the Son of Man and drink His blood, you have no life in you". (Jn 6:53). I eat in order to be rooted and established in Christ 'the true vine'. I will not be a reed in the wind of the world, but a column in God's Temple. I will be firm and fruitful in the true vine when Christ says, "I am the vine, you are the branches. He who abides in Me, and I in him, bears much fruit; for without Me you can do nothing." (Jn 15:5)

• You openly gave me your body to eat. Allow me to unite with you in secret. (St. Cyril Liturgy)

<u>5 We ascend to praise alongside angels and saints:</u>

"Holy, Holy, Holy …"

The church in heaven is the summit of the mount of Transfiguration. It is the place where we are in the presence of Jesus, His angels and saints, including the ever-virgin Saint Mary. In the house of the Lord we also meet St. Mark the evangelist and other famous saints…Then, we share with the angels saying 'Holy', which is the sole blessing repeatedly said by all those around the altar. Only the holy precious blood of the Lord can deliver us from evil. Thus, we instantly find ourselves in heaven saying, "You have brought my first fruit up to heaven", and "When we stand before your holy altar, we are counted among those standing in heaven".

6 We ascend to be filled with joy and peace

We ask the Lord to fill our hearts with joy and peace that we may be able to devote ourselves to good deeds. The world only fills us with sadness, often leading to despair and failure due to sin which is spiritual death.

During the Liturgy we desperately ask God to remember those who have not yet tasted the sweetness of His love. We also sympathise with the sick, imprisoned, oppressed, and suffering. We are at ease when we hear the reassurance of Jesus saying, "Come unto me you all who are weary and I give you rest... Peace I leave with you; my peace I give you. I do not give to you as the world gives. Do not let your hearts be troubled and do not be afraid (John 14:27) whereby we stand confidently before the Lord's altar, "I went with them to the house of God, with the voice of joy and praise..." (Ps 42:4)

We kneel before You, O' Lord and we thank You because You filled all of us with joy when You came into the world. Glory be to You, O' Lord. We come to You crying from our souls saying, "Purify us O Lord". The Priest also says "Purify us with Your Holy Spirit".

• Purity is union with God, whereby I say: You endowed me to drink the cup of Your blood in purity. Bless me so as to unite with Your purity secretly (St Cyril Liturgy)

7 We ascend to seek on behalf of the multitudes

Lord, who will feed these hungry souls? Not even 200 dinars

will be enough to buy food, neither do we have any to feed them... We believe that Your sacrifice will suffice to satisfy 5000 people not only physically but also spiritually and emotionally. No single soul will leave hungry, but rather each one will leave with a basket full of food.

Ascending to the house of the Lord is an ascent alongside the Lord Jesus, one step at a time. Thus, without leaning on Christ's arm it is impossible to ascend like the saints.

During His ascent on the way to the cross, Christ was followed by a range of people. One could ask which category of people do we belong to?

1. During the liturgy, do we weep out of ignorance (like the daughters of Jerusalem), weeping for everything except our sins? Then, the words of Jesus come to mind, "Daughters of Jerusalem, weep not for me, but weep for yourselves, and for your children." (Lk 23:28)

The Lord reveals to us that the route of ascension ought to be flooded by the tears of repentance and the realisation that the sacrifice on the altar is for the remission of sins.

2. Do we unwittingly compete among the rushing crowds who followed Christ? This is like those who attend the Liturgy as a mere routine habit completely unaware of the great blessings and the focus of the liturgy, which is the sacrifice of Crucifixion.

3. Do we communicate with our Lord in a senseless manner like the left-hand thief whose words were only focused on being rescued from the agony of the cross to regain physical

comfort? Often, our prayers are only concentrated on earthly things; such as food, work, exams …. despite knowing that God provides these to all people. We ought to bear in mind that the liturgy is a heavenly ascent rather than an earthly.

4. We ought to ascend with the right-hand thief who sought the heavenly life... This thief benefited from the sacrifice of the cross and offered a sincere repentance, beseeching the Lord to remember him in His Kingdom. The journey of ascension requires repentance combined with seeking the Kingdom.

5. Let us recall the image of Mary Magdalene and stand next to her at the foot of the cross where Christ's blood flowed... let us taste the sweetness of purification and the power of salvation through His blood…. let us be united in love with the One who hung on the cross, who liberated us from impurities …. Let us attend the Liturgy for the sake of being purified of our sins through His blood.

6. At the summit of our ascent, let us seek the blessing of the Virgin Mary and stand with her next to the Cross. Let us suffer with St. Mary as she suffered during the crucifixion of her Son, and later rejoiced for the salvation of the world. This is the most profound worship; experiencing the sufferings with Jesus Christ for the sake of the sinners, and later the infinite joy of salvation given by God with His sacrifice during the Liturgy.

7. Let us be cautious of foolish thoughts or inappropriate behaviour which we may commit ignorantly during the Liturgy, such as the soldier who stabbed Christ's body with a spear after His death. However, Christ emitted blood and

water from His side in order for us to believe. Let us control our thoughts and lift them up to the heights of heaven.

8. During the final stages of our ascent, let us ascend with the Lord towards the cross and turn our backs to the world that rejected and crucified Jesus. The cross became the summit of our ascension with Christ, whereby we begin the journey of our ministry.

It's inevitable that whoever ascended with Christ on the cross must have experienced the power of death to the world, and the power of the Resurrection and Ascension to Heaven. Through this triumphant power, one lowers himself to serve in the world and ascends again to Him.

DESCENT TO THE WORLD

1 The cross is the peak stage of ascent and death. From the cross we start the journey with Jesus alive within us...

2 We descend fully aware that the mysteries and blessings of the liturgy which we had received would not be possible for the world to understand.

We descend with the resolve that none of the lusts of the world would fill us with the blessings we had received, but on the contrary we realise that people of the world are deprived of the blessings. We descend cautiously, lest the world might rob us of what we had received.

• We descend in the company of our Lord Jesus, with love rather than the human law of "an eye for an eye". We love according to our communion and oneness with the divine nature, "....by which have been given to us exceedingly great and precious promises, that through these you may be partakers of the divine nature, having escaped the corruption that is in the world through lust." (2 Pet 1:4)

• We descend to the world with Christ's meekness and endurance to sufferings, rather than our human ability.

The martyrs and the bearers of the cross endured suffering beyond human ability due to the meekness of Jesus.

• We descend to the broken hearts of people to reassure and introduce them to the mystery of the great joy. We share with them what we had received ... We try to answer all the questions about the secret behind the joy and hope within us.

• We do not solve the problems of people, nor do we have the capacity within ourselves to do so. On the contrary, we begin our mission with the death of self and share the message of salvation through Christ who carries away the sins of the world. Our strength in our mission is in the meek Jesus, the quencher of all souls thirsting for Him.

• We are responsible to be a light to others in the world even though the world wearies us... We descend to the world like the descent of Noah's dove and return quickly to the Ark, which symbolises the Church.

• We descend to the world with Jesus and return quickly to the Lord's altar to obtain our living sustenance in this world. We ascend to continue in His divine love to satisfy our desires.

• Jesus continues ascending and descending with us for as

long as we are sojourners in this world.

In conclusion, the total number of times we ascend to the altar of the Lord becomes the force which elevates us to joyful eternity.

TRAINING

1 When we attend the Liturgy we should think about several issues; particularly our desires, needs, and our ascent with the Lord previously mentioned in our reflections.

2 When we descend from the Church, we do so holding the great message to the world about Jesus who is alive within us.

3 While we are in the world, we live with a sense of being foreigners in this world yearning to return to our Father's house

BEFORE THE SACRIFICE

• "Give unto the Lord the glory due unto his name: bring an offering, and come into his courts."(Ps 96:8)

• "Gather my saints together unto me; those that have made a covenant with me by sacrifice."(Ps 50:5)

• The Lamb is spiritual; but the knife is inanimate, non-corporal: this is the sacrifice which we are offering before you. (St. Gregory)

• Christians are Christ's light within humans - (Philokalia).

Thus, God became incarnate and was slain for us on the cross in the body which He took from us and resurrected with Him.

Through Christ's incarnation, God proclaimed the human race as being alive through the living God within us. Thus, the Liturgy of the Eucharist is the means for the continuity of Christ's slaying before us and living in Christ when we partake of His body.

When the priest takes the inanimate knife and fulfils the sacrifice before the eyes of our spiritual hearts, then our love for God grows to participate in the sacrifice of the Eucharist. Consequently, our belief in Christ is raised to participate in the sacrifice until death. Our spiritual struggle and keeping God's commandants raises us to be in Christ. In the Liturgy of St. Cyril it says, "Purify our inner being to be as pure as your only Son, He whom we are about to receive".

<u>Include your believers among your martyrs</u>

• When believers come to church they ought to take their inanimate knife of faith to use it for slaying the sacrifice of their love for Jesus. They offer their repentance to combat the lusts in their eyes and to cut off their faltering hands and feet. The believers become inspired by this supernatural power when they discover the inanimate knife which the priest uses to slaughter the lamb of God offered on the altar. The believers repeat with the prophet David saying," Gather my saints together unto me…"(Ps 50:5)

• The inanimate knife differs from a metal knife as it does not require manual effort but mere utterance. When we focus our minds on the sacrifice on the altar, the level of our belief is raised whereby it is easier to utter repentance saying, "I will not return to sinning.... I will sever the chains of this lust... I will uproot ...." This utterance before the sacrifice is actually separating and uprooting the world and its lusts. God's righteous people assemble in the church, offering their sacrifice together with the saints in heaven who previously offered their sacrifices to the Lord... Christ is slain on the altar for our sake in a covenant whereby we become "partners in the body of Christ"... All this takes place "in communion with Christ and partnership with Him". (Submission Prayer: Father St. Cyril)

1.The Sacrifice of our faith:
The faith of the whole Church

"Yes, and if I am being poured out as a drink offering on the sacrifice and service of your faith..."(Ph 2:17)

• When Christ offers an infinite sacrifice for our sake on the altar, and when the Priest uses an inanimate knife, our belief elevates to the infinite level of the slaughter whereby, "I can do all things through Christ who strengthens me."(Ph 4:13) Also, we are able to cast out into the sea all the mountain of sin which are sitting on our hearts. We are able to feel the infinite knife of the Holy Spirit and the infinite sacrifice we eat; we are able to overcome the world, the flesh, and death saying, "You are of God, little children, and have overcome them, because He who is in you is greater than he who is in the world."(1 Jn 4:4) ..."Our faith has allowed us to become victorious over the world. (1 Jn 5:4)

• This faith of offering was lived by Abraham who took his inanimate knife and slew his only son whom he loved. This same faith was lived by the martyrs who mortified their flesh and did not love the world, but rather rejected it and all its lusts.

• When the church stands before the divine sacrifice, the sole means is to elevate her children's faith. It is the faith which defies fear, pain, death and sadness, whereby the youth are able to triumph over the world and crucify its lusts. The church is triumphant with infinite power, thus, we are partake in this sacrifice of Christ.

2 - The sacrifice of our repentance and confession

• "Receive our repentance and confession on your sacred, pure and divine altar" [St. Basil's Liturgy]

• We repent many times and return to the same sin just as often. However, when we stand before the altar and bear in mind the sacrifice offered by both Abraham and Isaac, we can repent and be raised to the ultimate sacrifice of offering ourselves unto death. Also, it's very important that we, "resist sin to bloodshed" (Heb 12:4)

How do we repent till 'bloodshed'?

a) We stand before the altar saying, "My Lord Jesus, martyrs had offered You their blood, and those who lived in the wilderness offered You their whole lives. Now, I am offering You myself and repenting even if this may lead to suffering until death.

b) We offer this repentance to the priest that he may in turn say, "May You receive this confession and repentance on your divine, pure and sacred altar" (St. Basil). Our repentance touches the infinite nature of Christ's sacrifice, whereupon we sing joyously to the Lord, "You have loosed my bonds. I will offer to You the sacrifice of thanksgiving, (Ps 116:16)

• My Lord Jesus: give the church power in fulfilment of the priest's prayer, "include Your believers among Your martyrs".

<u>3 - The sacrifice of our will and our 'being'</u>

The Lord Jesus had sacrificed His will prior to being raised on the cross when He said, "nevertheless not My will, but Yours, be done." (Lk 22:24) Also, during the Liturgy before the invocation of the Holy Spirit and its conclusion the priest says, "I offer you the freedom of my will".

Whoever attends the Liturgy ought to sacrifice his will to God. We slaughter our will to acquire the one will of the whole Church, the will of Christ. When the Priest says, "we become one body and one spirit" it means that there is no division within the church. "I will freely sacrifice to You; I will praise Your name, O Lord, for it is good."(Ps 54:6)

<u>4 - The Sacrifice of our Bodies</u>

"I beseech you therefore, brethren, by the mercies of God, that you present your bodies a living sacrifice, holy, acceptable to God, which is your reasonable service. And do not be conformed to this world..."(Rom 12:1-2)

My Lord Jesus, You are offering before me your crucified body whereby my belief is strengthened through the life resulting from the crucifixion of the body in that I now offer You my body as a holy and living sacrifice. "And those who are Christ's have crucified [slain] the flesh with its passions and desires." (Gal 5:24)

My slain body does not live on bread alone, but with the living body of Christ slain on the altar. Consequently, no one is able to receive Christ's slain body unless they crucify their own body first. Standing before the altar during the liturgy is a total crucifixion of the desires of the flesh for the sake of professing Jesus alive within us. We live bearing the countenance of the Lord Jesus within our bodies, similar to martyrs.

5 - The Sacrifice of Joy and Thanksgiving

"The Mercy of Peace, Sacrifice of Praise" (Divine Liturgy)

Praise and joy in the church are linked to Christ's slaying. Thus, they praise joyfully around the slain Lamb, "saying with a loud voice: "Worthy is the Lamb who was slain" (Rev 5:12)

Hence, for as long as we are in church, we sing, "Praise the Lord! For it is good to sing praises to our God" (Ps 147:1). However, when the transformation of bread into the body of the Lord Jesus on the altar takes place, the prayer rises deeply to match the raising of the inanimate knife towards the spiritual Lamb... This stage kindles the feelings within us: we feel the mixed feelings of thanksgiving, joy and praise to the level of the sacrifice which has a special praise like the book of Revelation, "For You were slain, And have redeemed us to God by Your blood" (Rev 5:9)

* The Song of Freedom from Him who broke our shackles and I sacrifice to Him (Ps.115:7)

* The Song of Triumph from Him who triumphed over the

world (Jn 16:33).

* The Song Of Life from Him who said "so he who feeds on Me will live because of Me" (Jn.6:57).

* The Song of Joy..."Then I will go to the altar of God, To God my exceeding joy" (Ps.43:4).

During the Liturgy we reach a heavenly state of spiritual joy attainable only through the sacrifice of the Holy Spirit.

<u>6 - The Sacrifice of our love of Jesus</u>

Before He was crucified, our Lord Jesus submitted Himself to sufferings beyond human endurance. Thus, in the liturgy immediately before the invocation of the Holy Spirit and the inanimate knife, the church recites "... and as we are in the process of remembrance of His holy sufferings..." because at this stage we recall Him who was "taken to the slaughter"... The priest continues, "He was oppressed and He was afflicted, He was led as a lamb to the slaughter, and as a sheep before its shearers is silent, so He opened not His mouth." (Is 53:7) We pause to reflect upon Him whose face was spat upon and whose back was scourged, "Let him give his cheek to the one who strikes him, And be full of reproach". (Lam 3:30). "I have become the ridicule of all my people - Their taunting song all the day. He has filled me with bitterness, He has made me drink wormwood."(Lam 3:14)

How can one not be heartbroken during the remembrance of our Lord's sufferings when He said, "My soul is overwhelmed with sorrow to the point of death."? He ascended on the cross to free Adam from Hades, and also was slaughtered, descended from the altar to the Hades of our hearts, souls and bodies, and liberate us from the sins of the world.

The liturgy is the perfect time where we can open our hearts to receive Christ's glory. The sacrifice on the altar is a spiritual fire which kindles our hearts with love towards Christ who was slain for us. If this fire ignites to kindle all our feelings of love, then we are able to offer our feelings of love as a sacrifice to Christ our Saviour.

7 - The Sacrifice of Peace and Love

"Walk in Love. Therefore be imitators of God as dear children. And walk in love, as Christ also has loved us and given Himself for us, an offering and a sacrifice to God for a sweet-smelling aroma." (Eph 5:2)

"Therefore if you bring your gift to the altar, and there remember that your brother has something against you, leave your gift there before the altar, and go your way. First be reconciled to your brother, and then come and offer your gift." (Mt 5:23-24)

Our love and tolerance of others is limited due to our human ability. However, after Christ's sacrifice, this limit can now extend to Christ's endurance on the Cross. We now have grace to love and endure others to the end, similar to what St. Stephen said, " Lord, do not charge them with this sin." (Acts 7:60) Reaching this stage of sacrifice is a beautiful fragrance offered to God that is transferred to others.

8 - The Sacrifice of Charity

"But do not forget to do good and to share, for with such

sacrifices God is well pleased."(Heb 13:16)

When almsgiving is done with love and gladly offered in the name of Jesus, it turns into self-denial, which is a sacrifice in itself. The apostle Peter had denied himself for the needy, sacrificing even his own life.

When an offering is made to the slain who became poor in order to enrich us, we can become the fragrance of God, similar to the offering of the widow who gave her last two coins. In the litany of the oblations the priest says "… Receive them upon Your holy rational altar…"

9 - The Sacrifice of the Broken Spirit

"The sacrifices of God are a broken spirit" (Ps 51:17)

The sacrifices of God due to His infinite love and pure blood wash us and reveal our sins. There is no moment comparable to the moment of when the inanimate knife is laid on the altar for our sake … this stage of becoming 'broken spirits'. Therefore, it is the one who offers God the sacrifice of the broken spirit who is worthy of partaking of His body which is broken for the remission of our sins.

"Give to the LORD the glory due His name; Bring an offering, and come into His courts."(Ps 96:8)

Therefore, when we are at the doorstep of the house of Lord and reach the altar, we ought to offer the Lord our sacrifice: our only son whom we love. Then we can hold our spiritual inanimate knife and be slaughtered in the name of the Lord, "who was crucified for us"… We crucify our will and lusts, and even offer ourselves to be slaughtered for His name's sake…

the ultimate sacrifice and love of our faith. We do good for all, including giving to whoever is in need. We lead a life of humility until we hear our Lord's call, "Gather My saints together to Me, Those who have made a covenant with Me by sacrifice." (Ps 50:5).

Joining the Lord means that He offers us His blood, the covenant of His love, and invites us to His banquet, "Come, eat of my bread, and drink of the wine I have mixed."(Prov 9:5) Thus we are among our saintly fathers, holding their relics assembling around the altar in a magnificent and heavenly procession exemplifying the sacrifice they offered when they were in the body:

* Our Ever Virgin: a sword pierced through St. Mary's heart and she shared in her Son's Sacrifice

* John the Baptist: offered his head for the sake of the Truth.

* Mark, apostle and martyr: He served Christ to the last drop of his blood in the streets of Alexandria

* Severus, Dioscorus and Athanasius: they defended the faith until death

* Peter the Seal of Martyrs: was slaughtered for the sake of his people, similar to the One who was slain for the sake of the world.

* St. John Chrysostom: was slaughtered because of his impartiality.

* The 318 and 150 and 200 assembled in the three ecumenical councils: all of them were witnesses to the Lord through their apostolic faith.

* Saints Anthony and Paula: abandoned everything and followed Christ to the end. They died to the world and lived in the wilderness, caves and deserts of the earth because of their great love to Christ.

* Anba Macarius: endured oppression and humiliation for the sake of Jesus who was despised and mocked.

* Anba Pishoy: carried the weak and endured their burdens until he saw the suffering Christ in the flesh.

* Maximous and Domadious: counted themselves martyrs in prayer for Christ.

* The strong Moses the Black: offered repentance and fought sin until death.

* The forty-nine martyrs: preferred to be slain for Christ rather than temporal life on earth.

Thus, these are the saints who assemble around the sacrifice; "Gather My saints together to Me, who have made a covenant with Me by sacrifice."

A M E N

www.ingramcontent.com/pod-product-compliance
Lightning Source LLC
Chambersburg PA
CBHW021913040426
42447CB00007B/838